✳ CONTENTS

Our Family Tree

Our most treasured
heirlooms are our sweet
family memories.

~AUTHOR UNKNOWN

Your great-great grandparents (my grandparents)

NAME, BIRTH DATE & PLACE

NAME, BIRTH DATE & PLACE

NAME, BIRTH DATE & PLACE

NAME, BIRTH DATE & PLACE

Your great-grandparents (my parents)

NAME

BIRTH DATE & PLACE

NAME

BIRTH DATE & PLACE

Your grandparents (ME)

NAME

BIRTH DATE & PLACE

NAME

BIRTH DATE & PLACE

Your parents

NAME

BIRTH DATE & PLACE

NAME

BIRTH DATE & PLACE

You, my grandchild

NAME

BIRTH DATE & PLACE

Introduction

Memories for My Grandchild is literally the gift of a lifetime—notably *your* lifetime. Once completed, it will contain information that your grandchild will treasure. The book will tell your life story; it will answer your grandchild's questions about his or her roots, and provide an invaluable context for his or her own life.

Divided into nine chapters, each containing clear prompts and questions, *Memories for My Grandchild* provides an easy framework into which you record your living history. Each chapter ends with a page for photos, memorabilia, and free writing.

The idea is to allow your grandchild to know who you are—besides, of course, being their grandma or grandpa. It's your chance to inspire the next generation with your life experience and accomplishments.

There's also a lot of fun in learning about your day-to-day life, especially as you grew up. Could you really see a feature film for under $2? What movie star made your heart quicken? Did you have a favorite hobby? Who was the most significant world leader in your lifetime? Is it true that as much as things change, they stay the same? Your life provides the most fascinating history lesson your grandchild will ever have.

Most valuable, though, is what your grandchild will learn about *you*. The pages that follow will help reveal you as an evolving person, living life in full color. By providing your life with context and texture, you will give your grandchild a better appreciation of who you really are. Though separated by a generation, the links between you will emerge from the pages. At times your grandchild will see him or herself in you; and through your lens, he or she will surely see interesting things about the world and about family. The connections are what matter most.

Feel free to skip over any questions that don't apply. And be sure to check your modesty at the door. The best memoirs are the ones that are unedited, and come straight from the heart.

Your Birth and Background

Once upon a time, in a far-off (or not so far-off) land, your story began, Grandparent. Chapter One is, appropriately, a place to record important facts about your heritage. Answer any questions you can about your roots, and help fill in the blanks for your grandchild and for generations to come.

Your First Days

What is your birth date?

Where were you born?

Do you know your birth weight and length?

What was your home address?

What is your full given name?

Were you named after anyone? Explain.

What were you called? If you had a nickname, who came up with it and why?

Are there any stories you were told about your birth?

Was there a welcoming celebration for you, religious or otherwise?

Was there anything else notable about your babyhood?

Parents

Where were your parents born? Where did they grow up?

Did your parents or grandparents emigrate from another country? If so, where were they from and when did they emigrate? Where did they settle and why? What do you know about their traditions?

What is the meaning of your family's last names?

How would you describe your mother?

Does one special memory about your mother stand out?

When you were little, what did you like most about your mother?

How would you describe your father?

_____

_____

_____

_____

_____

_____

_____

Does one special memory about your father stand out?

_____

_____

_____

_____

_____

_____

_____

When you were little, what did you like most about your father?

_____

_____

_____

_____

_____

_____

In the early family days, what did your parents value most?

When you were a child, what kind of work did your parents do for a living?

● Mother:

● Father:

What interests or hobbies did they have?

● Mother:

● Father:

Name a characteristic you inherited from your mother:

Name a characteristic you inherited from your father:

What were your parents' spiritual or religious beliefs and affiliations when you were young? Did they change?

Did they have any special expressions you remember them saying often?

What was at least one important thing you learned, or learned to do or appreciate …

- … from your mother?

- … from your father?

Grandparents

What do you remember about your own grandparents? (For example, where were they born? Where did they grow up? What did they do for work and enjoyment? What things did you do with them? What did you call them? How many children did they have?)

● On your mother's side:

● On your father's side:

PHOTOS • MEMORIES • MEMORABILIA • MUSINGS

CHAPTER TWO

Your Childhood and Teenage Years

Yes, "Kids are kids," as they say, but not when the kids in question are Grandma or Grandpa! There's something utterly fascinating and absolutely transporting in picturing a grandparent as a real-life child. So step out of the snapshots of those family photo albums and present yourself to your grandchild in vivid 3-D.

When you were a child, who were you told you resembled, if anyone?

What was your home address?

What do you remember about your home?

What do you remember about your room?

What language or languages were spoken in your home?

Did you have a "best friend?" Describe.

_____

_____

_____

Who were your other close friends?

_____

_____

_____

_____

What were your favorite hobbies or activities?

_____

_____

_____

_____

_____

Did you prefer playing inside or outside . . . or both?

_____

_____

What games did you like to play?

_____

_____

_____

Did you have a favorite toy or special "something?"

Did you take music or any other lessons?

Did you get an allowance? If so, how much?

What did you spend it on?

What was your family car like?

Did you collect anything?

What was your favorite food?

What was your favorite *home-cooked* food?

Was there anything you hated to eat?

What was your favorite ice cream flavor?

What was your favorite holiday and why?

What was the most memorable gift you received?

What were your favorite books?

What were your favorite radio or TV shows?

What were your favorite movies?

Did you have a favorite TV or movie star?

Did you have a favorite singer or group?

Did you regularly listen or watch with anyone? With whom?

What was your favorite spectator sport?

Who was your favorite athlete?

What was the most memorable event you attended?

Did you have a favorite color?

What were some of the silly (or naughty) things you remember doing?

What scared you?

How did your parents discipline you if you did something wrong?

What were your chores or responsibilities?

What did you want to be when you grew up?

Siblings

List your siblings, in order of their births:

What recollections about them stand out? What did you do for fun together?

Were there relatives with whom you were particularly close? Which ones? And what made them special to you? Where did they live? Near you?

When you were a teenager, who were your close friends?

Who or what were your top:

- Musical groups/singers? How did you listen to them (LPs, cassettes, radio, live concerts, etc.)?

- Books?

- Magazines?

- Radio or TV programs?

- Movies?

- Movie stars?

- Dances?

- Sports teams?

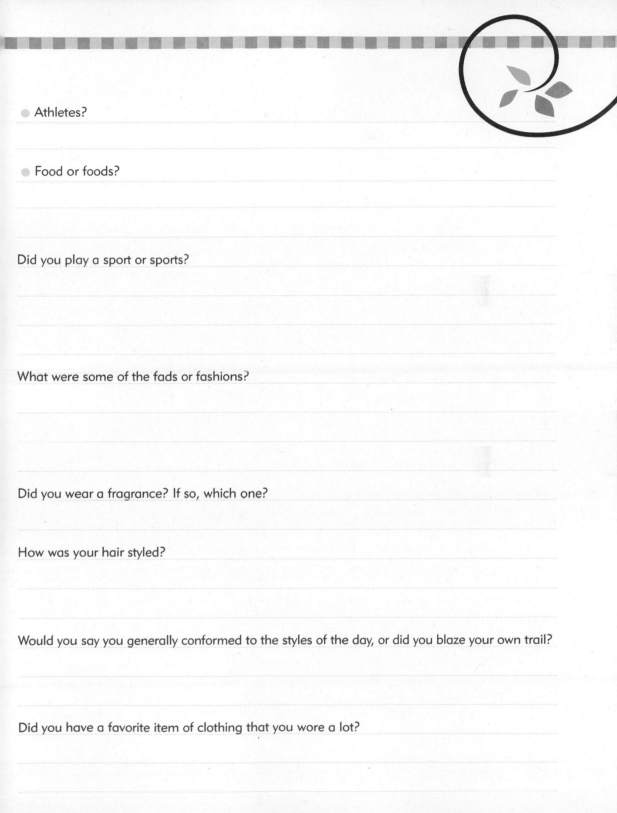

Athletes?

Food or foods?

Did you play a sport or sports?

What were some of the fads or fashions?

Did you wear a fragrance? If so, which one?

How was your hair styled?

Would you say you generally conformed to the styles of the day, or did you blaze your own trail?

Did you have a favorite item of clothing that you wore a lot?

What stores did you shop in? Whom did you shop with?

Who did you dream of being (or looking) like?

Did you have any idols/heroes?

What was the approximate cost of:

- A candy bar?

- A movie ticket?

- A postage stamp?

- A phone call at a pay phone?

What were some expressions teens frequently used?

Did you live in the same house throughout your teen years? If not, how many times did you move, and from where to where?

Did you have a favorite room in your house or getaway place where you regularly met friends?

As a teen, how did you get along with your parents?

● Mother:

● Father:

Did you work? If so, what did you do? How much did you earn?

Were you involved in any causes, political or otherwise?

Did you learn to drive as a teen? If so, who taught you? What car did you learn on?

Did you have any pets? If so, what kind, and what were their names?

Did you have a favorite pet? Describe.

Where did you go on family vacations or holidays?

Do you have any special vacation recollections?

How were your summers spent?

Did you have any special family traditions, including holidays or other "magical times?"
With whom were they spent?

What were your family's everyday rituals (e.g., bedtime reading; dinnertime; listening to the radio or watching TV together; playing particular games together; prayer)?

As a young person, would you say you were (circle one and explain):

- Quiet

- Chatty

- Somewhere in between

Describe your personality.

Were there hardships you had to overcome as a youngster? If so, how did you overcome them?

What modern conveniences or technologies were not part of your early years?

What one word might have been used by people to describe you as a child or teen?

Why?

PHOTOS • MEMORIES • MEMORABILIA • MUSINGS

CHAPTER THREE

Your Student Life

Whether you were "rah-rah" or "nah-nah," school was a significant part of your life. This chapter provides a chance for you to write the book on your education, letting your grandchild see just how you got to know so much! Whether you feel you owe it all to your alma mater, to life experience, or both, your grandchild will surely learn a thing or two from your candid thoughts on this important subject.

What kindergarten and elementary schools did you attend and where were they located?

When were you a student there?

Did you have any favorite teachers? If so, what made them special?

What were your favorite subjects and activities?

Did anything give you particular difficulty?

Were you in any school concerts or plays?

Did you play any sports in elementary school?

What did you generally do after school?

Do you have any especially fond recollections of your early school experience?

If you attended religious school, where was it, and what did you study? How old were you?

What was the name of your middle school, and where was it located?

What years did you attend?

What were your favorite subjects?

What subjects came the most easily to you?

What subjects gave you the most difficulty?

Did you have any favorite or memorable teachers? If so, what made them special?

Were you involved in any extracurricular activities or sports?

Were you a member of any school clubs?

What was your social life like?

What was the most memorable thing you learned in middle school?

What were the highlights of your middle school years?

How would you describe your overall middle school experience?

What high school did you attend, and where was it located?

What years did you attend?

What were your favorite subjects?

What subjects came the most easily to you?

What subjects gave you the most difficulty?

Did you have any favorite or memorable teachers? If so, what made them special or memorable?

Were you involved in any extracurricular activities or sports?

Did you ever get involved in horseplay or hijinks?

Were you a member of any school clubs?

What was your social life like? Did kids date?

What was the most important or useful thing you learned in high school?

What was the least useful thing you learned in high school?

What were the highlights of your high school years?

What were your goals after high school?

Generally, do you remember your high school experience as being fun or difficult, or a combination of the two?

Did you attend college or trade school, or join the military? If so, where and when?

What did you study, and what was your major?

Did you live at home or away? Describe your living situation.

Who were your close friends?

Were you a member of a sorority or fraternity or other social club?

Did you graduate with a degree (or honors)? If so, in what?

What were the highlights of your post-high school experience?

Did you pursue any other education?

Do you have any regrets about your education?

Do you have any general thoughts about education that may be helpful to future generations?

PHOTOS • MEMORIES • MEMORABILIA • MUSINGS

CHAPTER FOUR

Love and Marriage

Your grandkids would love to know
more about their grandfather and
grandmother and how it all began.
After all, your relationship generated
a whole new branch of the family tree.
Please provide as many details as
you can.

How, where, and when did you meet your spouse?

How old were you?

What did you find most appealing about your future spouse?

How long did you date before you decided to get married?

Did you get formally engaged? If so, where and when?

Was there a bridal shower? If so, who hosted it and where was it held?

Where and when did you get married? What was the wedding like?

What did you wear?

Who were some members of your bridal party?

Did you go on a honeymoon? If so, where, and for how long?

Do you have any honeymoon stories, funny or otherwise, to share?

Is (or was) yours a marriage of many years? If so, to what do you attribute your long-lasting relationship? (If not, why do you think it did not last?)

Where was your first home together?

When did you first meet your spouse's family and what were your impressions of them?

What were your favorite things to do together as a couple?

Who have been your special friends as a couple through the years?

Did you get married more than once? If so, to whom?

Do you have any stories to share about your marriage or adventures with your spouse?

PHOTOS • MEMORIES • MEMORABILIA • MUSINGS

CHAPTER FIVE

Parenthood and Family Life

Here's where you took that momentous first step on the way to grandparenting: parenthood! These years were undoubtedly jam-packed with activity, calling upon total love, patience, energy, empathy, dedication, and the most extraordinary juggling skills imaginable. This is the place to reveal how you raised your grandchild's parent.

Please list full names and birth dates of your child or children.

Did you keep baby books?

Was there anything notable about the birth(s)?

Did you name your child(ren) after anyone?

If there are godparents, who are they?

Where did you raise your family? What was your home address, and what was your home like?

Can you share a story about your child(ren) or a recollection of any childhood antics?

What are some notable traits of your grandchild's parent (as a baby, child, teen, or adult)?

What were some of the special things you did as a family?

How were summers and vacations spent?

Were there any trips you remember most vividly?

Were there any favorite meals you traditionally prepared? Can you share a recipe?

Were there any special friends your family spent a lot of time with?

Did religion play a big role in your family's life?

What would you say were the most important values you tried to instill in your child(ren)?

What was the best part of raising a family?

What was the trickiest part of raising a family?

Based on your own experience, do you have any words of wisdom or advice on parenting?

CHAPTER SIX

Work and Community

What you choose to do with your time says a lot about you. Whether you raised your children full time, worked outside the home, or both, your contributions to your household and community have been invaluable— and a big part of your life story.

What was your very first job? How old were you? Describe.

Are you employed? Retired?

What is (or was) your occupation?

For whom and where have you worked?

Have you had any special mentors?

What was your best job, so far, and why?

What was your worst job, so far, and why?

Do you have any ideas or tips about choosing a career?

What business or investment advice can you offer that you may have learned from your successes and/or failures?

_____

_____

_____

_____

_____

_____

Have you had any involvement in the military? If so, what, where, and when?

_____

_____

_____

Have you been actively involved as a volunteer in community organizations or causes? If so, which and what kind of work have you done? At what times in your life?

_____

_____

_____

_____

CHAPTER SEVEN

Religion and Spirituality

How do you nurture your soul? This chapter will let you share with your grandchild your beliefs about religion and spirituality, and the role they've played in your life to date.

Do you have a religious affiliation?

How do you practice your religion or spirituality?

Is religion or spirituality a driving force in your life?

Are you a member of any congregation or religious organization?

Do you have a favorite prayer or scripture passage?

Did you say a special bedtime prayer as a child? If so, what was it?

Did you say a special bedtime prayer with your own child or children?

Do you say a prayer before meals?

Do you have a favorite piece of sacred music?

What religious rituals or traditions are most important to you?

Did your religious or spiritual beliefs change or evolve at any point in your life? How, and what prompted the change?

Has religion or spirituality helped you get through difficult times? If so, please describe.

What was your most memorable religious or spiritual experience?

What kind of religious or spiritual training did you give your children?

CHAPTER EIGHT

Life and Living

The odds and ends of everyday life—
like the objects on your night table right
now—can offer the truest picture of the real
you. This chapter is all about the world
according to Grandma or Grandpa.
Your responses to the questions that
follow will help reveal what makes up
who you really are.

Think fast and simply jot down the
answers that come to mind.

How old are you now?

What do you do for fun?

What or who makes you laugh?

List three or more things a perfect day would entail.

Of what personal achievements are you most proud?

What was the most difficult thing you've had to overcome, and how did you overcome it?

What is the best way to deal with a bully or difficult person?

Who are your best and/or oldest friends?

What's the most important thing you can do to nurture a good, lasting friendship?

Where have you traveled that's been most memorable? Describe.

Have you enjoyed collecting anything? Explain.

What have been the biggest cultural or fashion trends in your lifetime?

What's the oddest thing you've ever seen or heard in your life?

What's the most significant breakthrough, discovery, or invention you've witnessed (technological, medical, or other)?

What invention has directly affected or enhanced your life the most?

Who was the first national leader you voted for?

What are the most pivotal national or international events that have occurred in your lifetime?

What is your most vivid historical recollection?

Is there a cause or issue that is, or has been, particularly important to you?

What's the most adventurous thing you've done, so far?

What's the most exciting encounter you've had with a famous or noteworthy person?

Do you speak more than one language? If so, which one(s) are you fluent in or familiar with?

What skills or talents have you tried to develop?

Have you recently attended any lectures, courses, or workshops?

How do you make a tough decision?

How do you overcome a fear?

What advice do people seek from you?

What book are you reading now, if any?

What is on your night table or desk as you are writing this?

What would the menu of your perfect meal feature?

What are your favorite kinds of stores? Are you a bargain hunter?

If you had a motto, what would it be?

Your theme song would be:

What would your friends say is "so you"?

Is there anything you'd like to share that your grandchild might not know about you?

Fill in the blanks

I believe in _____ in moderation.

I believe in _____ in abundance.

I don't believe in _____

_____

_____

Something I wish I'd done more of: _____

_____

_____

_____

Something I wish I'd done less of: _____

_____

_____

_____

Something I still wish to do: _____

_____

_____

_____

One food I cannot stand: _____

_____

Circle one:

I like to drink: coffee   tea   none   both   other:

I am a: morning person   night owl

It's not easy being

It's great to be

The place where I get my best ideas:

Always have a   on hand.

You can never have enough

People make too big a deal about

People don't make a big enough deal about

In my life, everyone thought I shouldn't _____ , but I'm so glad I did, because

_____

_____

Something I admire most in others:

_____

_____

Something I admire most in myself:

_____

_____

_____

Something I really used to dislike, but now I like:

_____

_____

_____

_____

The best thing about being my age:

_____

_____

_____

_____

My most featured role in life has been as a

_____

_____

_____

_____

Who or what are your top picks, and why?

Actors:

Writers:

Books (or type of book):

Magazines (or type of magazine) or newspapers:

Web sites:

Musicians, singers, or bands (or type of music):

Artists or works of art:

Journalists or news anchors:

Movies (or type of movie):

_____

_____

_____

_____

TV shows:

_____

_____

_____

Radio shows:

_____

_____

_____

Kinds of show (opera, ballet, movie, play, musical):

_____

_____

_____

Public figures:

_____

_____

Comedians:

_____

_____

Spectator sports:

_____

Athletes:

Sports to play:

Games to play:

Charities, organizations, or causes:

Day of the week:

Season:

Time of day:

Holiday (describe):

Meal (describe):

Comfort foods:

Pick-me-ups:

Desserts:

Ice cream flavor (has it stayed the same since childhood?):

Drinks:

Outfits or designers:

Color (has it stayed the same since childhood?):

Expressions or words:

Way to communicate (by phone, writing letters, e-mail, or in person):

Machines or gadgets:

Extravagance:

Restaurants:

Hotels:

Place in the world:

Rainy day activity:

Sunny day activity:

Animals:

Decade or age:

CHAPTER NINE

Grandparenthood

When the grand stork arrived, he brought the most special of deliveries! It's difficult to put into words the loving bond between a grandparent and grandchild. Your grandchild cherishes having you as a guardian angel, whose love is boundless and unconditional. **Here's where you write directly to him or her, rounding out your life story in the most meaningful and personal of ways.**

*If you're writing this with more than one grandchild in mind,
here's ample space for you to personalize your answers for each.*

What I remember most about your arrival:

What you were like as a baby:

Pet name I have for you, and how it came to be:

Special name you have for me, and how it came to be:

A story I remember from your earliest years:

Similarities between you and your parent (my child):

Things you seem to have inherited from other family members:

Something you may have inherited from me:

Some special qualities I see in you:

Some of our favorite activities we do together:

When you visit, you like to:

Things you do that make me smile or laugh:

_____
_____
_____
_____
_____
_____
_____

Things you do that make me proud:

_____
_____
_____
_____
_____
_____
_____

My hopes and dreams for your future:

_____
_____
_____
_____
_____
_____

PHOTOS • MEMORIES • MEMORABILIA • MUSINGS

PHOTOS · MEMORIES · MEMORABILIA · MUSINGS